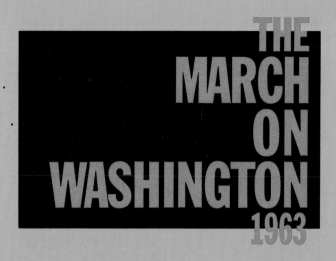

THE
MARCH
ON
WASHINGTON
1963

THE
MARCH ON WASHINGTON
1963 GATHERING TO BE HEARD

BY TRICIA ANDRYSZEWSKI

Spotlight on American History
The Millbrook Press • Brookfield, Connecticut

"Dream Deferred" from *The Panther and the Lash*, by Langston Hughes.
Copyright 1951 by Langston Hughes. Reprinted by permission of
Alfred A. Knopf Inc.

Library of Congress Cataloging-in-Publication Data
Andryszewski, Tricia, 1956–
The March on Washington, 1963 : gathering to be heard / Tricia
Andryszewski.
p.   cm. — (Spotlight on American history)
Includes bibliographical references (p.   ) and index.
Summary: Recounts the historical antecedents and events leading up
to the March on Washington in 1963, led by Martin Luther King, Jr.,
and other prominent African American leaders in their quest for
equal civil rights.
ISBN 0–7613–0009–0 (lib. bdg.)
1. March on Washington for Jobs and Freedom, Washington, D.C.,
1963—Juvenile literature.   2. Civil rights demonstrations—
Washington (D.C.)—History—20th century—Juvenile literature.
3. Afro-Americans—Civil rights—Juvenile literature.   [1. March on
Washington for Jobs and Freedom, Washington, D.C., 1963.   2. Civil
rights demonstrations.   3. Afro-Americans—Civil rights.]
I. Title.   II. Series.
F200.A55   1996   323.1′196073—dc20   96–1217   CIP   AC

Contents

Introduction
"I Have a Dream" 9

Chapter One
A Dream Deferred 11

Chapter Two
A Growing Movement 16

Chapter Three
Planning the March 23

Chapter Four
The Day of the March 34

Chapter Five
At the Lincoln Memorial 43

Chapter Six
After the March 53

Notes 59
Further Information 62
Index 63

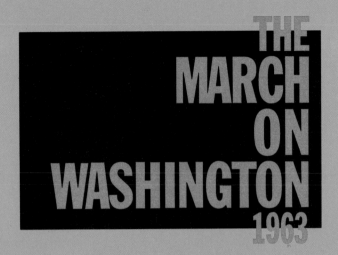

THE
MARCH
ON
WASHINGTON
1963

Martin Luther King, Jr. greeting some of the many marchers who gathered on August 28, 1963, to demonstrate for equal civil rights.

"I Have a Dream"

It was late in the afternoon of a hot August day in Washington, D.C. People were tired from a long day of traveling and then listening to hours of speeches. But the huge crowd facing the Lincoln Memorial applauded a long welcome when the man they most wanted to hear—the Reverend Martin Luther King, Jr.—stood up to speak to them.

"I am happy to join with you today in what will go down in history as the greatest demonstration for freedom in the history of our nation," King began. Speaking for just under nineteen minutes, he closed by setting aside his prepared speech and improvising the words that history would best remember him by: "I have a dream," he said, "that my four little children will one day live in a nation where they will not be judged by the color of their skin, but by the content of their character. . . .

"And when we allow freedom to ring . . . we will be able to speed up that day when all of God's children, black men and white men, Jews and Gentiles, Protestants and Catholics, will be able to join hands and sing in the words of the old Negro spiritual, 'Free at last! Free at last! Thank God Almighty, we are free at last!' " [1]

What happens to a dream deferred?
Does it dry up
Like a raisin in the sun?
Or fester like a sore—
And then run?
Does it stink like rotten meat
Or crust and sugar over—
Like a syrupy sweet?
Maybe it just sags
Like a heavy load.
Or does it explode?

LANGSTON HUGHES

A Dream Deferred

In 1963, less than a century after slavery was abolished in the United States, black Americans were far from "free at last."

In 1865 the North's victory in the Civil War led to the Thirteenth Amendment to the Constitution, which made slavery illegal all across America. Black Americans had high hopes for the future. In the years right after the Civil War (1865–1877), the U.S. federal government tried to give freed slaves throughout the South some of the rights and privileges enjoyed by white citizens. White Southerners so strongly opposed this effort, which was called Reconstruction, that by 1877 the U.S. government had mostly abandoned it. For many decades, it was primarily left up to the state governments to ensure the rights of their black citizens.

Segregation and inequality were written into state law and practiced as common custom especially, but not only, in the South. As a result, black Americans became second-class citizens. Whites and blacks in many states were forbidden to marry each other. Schools were segregated—white children went to different schools than black children, schools that had more books and better buildings. Most black children got such poor educations that the only work they could ever hope to be qualified for was unskilled, poorly paid, backbreaking labor. Even well-educated blacks found that good jobs were closed to them. And because few blacks possessed either land or tools with which to make a living, most remained dependent on white landowners and businessmen for jobs and could ill afford to complain about harsh or unfair treatment.

The highest court in the land, the Supreme Court of the United States, time after time allowed state discrimination against black citizens. In one of these decisions, in a case called *Plessy* v. *Ferguson* (1896), the Supreme Court ruled that it was legal to have "separate but equal" facilities for blacks and whites. Blacks could legally be forbidden from using train cars or toilets or lunch counters labeled "whites only." In practice, the separate facilities set up for blacks were usually far from "equal" to those set up for whites. The state and local laws that spelled out how blacks were to be segregated from whites were called Jim Crow laws, named after a slang term for black people.

Blacks throughout the South were also generally prevented from voting. The U.S. Constitution after the Civil War officially guaranteed black males the right to vote, which would have given blacks some power in shaping their laws and government. Nonetheless, white Southerners put into place many rules designed to disqualify blacks from voting. In some places, people who wanted to vote had to take reading tests that few blacks had adequate education to pass. In many places, white election officials simply cheated, refusing to count black votes.

White Southerners insisted that they were justified in using whatever means were necessary to keep blacks under tight control. "This is a white man's country, and white men must govern it," was how Benjamin R. Tillman, a white senator from South Carolina, put it. Addressing the Senate in 1907, Tillman said:

Look at our environment in the South, surrounded, and in a very large number of counties and in two States outnumbered, by the negroes—engulfed, as it were, in a black flood of semi-barbarians. . . . Some of them have just enough education to be able to read, but not always to understand what they read. Their minds are those of children, while they have the passions and strength of men. Taught that they are oppressed, and with breasts pulsating with hatred of the whites, the younger generation of negro men are roaming over the land, passing back and forth without hindrance, and with no possibility of adequate police protection to the communities in which they are residing.[1]

Violence walked with these ideas. During the late 1800s and early 1900s, dozens of blacks were lynched each year—killed by mobs of white people, often by hanging from a tree. Some of those killed were accused of crimes, but taken from jail and killed before they could have a trial. Others were just in the wrong place at the wrong time. In these Southern communities, no black person was ever entirely safe from attack.

By 1914, however, change was afoot. World War I cut the flow of white immigrants from Europe to the United States. This opened up new opportunities for the many black Americans who migrated to cities, mostly in the North, to take jobs that only a few years earlier would have gone to white Europeans. Segregation and discrimination were practiced in the North, too, but on the whole were less extreme there than in the South. Although frictions between whites and the black newcomers sparked a wave of race riots after the end of the war in 1918 through the early 1920s, most blacks stayed in their new communities.

Job opportunities for blacks and whites dried up in the Great Depression of the 1930s. In response, the "New Deal" programs

Although segregation and discrimination against blacks were still legal and commonplace in the 1930s, President Franklin D. Roosevelt's New Deal benefited black Americans.

created by President Franklin D. Roosevelt provided jobs, training, housing, and other services, and many blacks benefited from these programs. In general, Roosevelt and his administration's attitudes toward blacks were more inclusive and less discriminatory than those of earlier presidents. Black Americans were encouraged that they were becoming first-class citizens.

In the 1940s, job opportunities for all Americans increased once again when the country mobilized for World War II. More than a million black Americans served (in segregated units) in all branches of the armed forces during the war. Black workers at home were hired for jobs that in the past had never been open to them.

Black Americans were no longer mostly isolated on Southern farms. They had more opportunities and freedoms than they had ever enjoyed before. But lynchings continued to terrorize blacks in many areas. Segregation was still mostly legal, and customary in various ways and with various effects in different parts of the country. Blacks still were denied the right to vote throughout the South.

In the 1950s and 1960s, however, blacks and sympathetic whites joined together to nurture a growing movement to press for equal civil rights for black Americans.

A Growing Movement

Black Americans had been working for change all along, since the Civil War and even before. Even the idea of marching on Washington to demand equality, as they finally did in August of 1963, was nothing new.

Asa Philip Randolph, known as A. Philip Randolph, had first come up with the idea for a march on Washington to demand jobs and desegregation in 1941. Randolph had been a civil rights and labor leader for many years, founding the Brotherhood of Sleeping Car Porters in 1925 and then steering this union of railroad workers through the tough years of the Great Depression. In 1941, although military spending for World War II was giving a great boost to the economy, black workers were still the last to be hired, and many remained unemployed. Randolph told President Roosevelt that he was planning a massive march on Washington to demand more jobs for black workers in government offices and in the defense industry. In response, Roosevelt signed an executive order spelling out rules for nondiscrimination in areas that Randolph and his supporters had specified. Randolph called off his march. But he didn't forget about it.

In 1955, Rosa Parks was arrested for refusing to give up her seat on the bus to a white passenger. The Supreme Court later banned segregation on the city's public-transportation vehicles.

Blacks in Montgomery, Alabama, boycotted the city's bus system for one year to protest Rosa Parks's arrest. Churches and individuals organized car pools to provide the many boycotters with needed transportation.

During the 1950s, black Americans in the South (where Jim Crow laws were still in effect) began to try new, more aggressive tactics for winning freedom from discrimination. In 1955, Rosa Parks was arrested for refusing to give her seat to a white passenger and to move to the back of the bus, as black passengers were required to do in Montgomery, Alabama. Mrs. Parks's arrest set off a year-long boycott by blacks of the city's bus system, led by a young, recently ordained Baptist minister—the Reverend Martin Luther King, Jr. Inspired by the example of India's leader Mahatma Gandhi, King believed in nonviolent direct action (like a boycott) and passive resistance as tools to fight segregation and discrimination. King's powerful and insistent nonviolent tactics worked in Montgomery. Federal courts eventually ordered the bus system to treat its black patrons more fairly and declared segregation on buses unconstitutional. In addition, the nationally publicized boycott focused America's attention on civil rights. And the boycott's success encouraged other civil rights activists to try King's nonviolent tactics, boldly and bravely, in other places.

In 1960, young activists began to stage "sit-in" protests at whites-only lunch counters and other public facilities across the South. (Black customers who were refused service would sit down and refuse to leave.) In 1961, busloads of black and white "Freedom Riders" began to make trips through the South, seeking to make integrated use of bus terminals and other travel facilities. Civil rights lawyers continued to push for the admission of black students to previously all-white schools. (The Supreme Court in 1954, in *Brown* v. *Topeka Board of Education*, had ruled that separate schools for black and white students were "inherently unequal" and therefore illegal. Nonetheless, black students had to go to court again and again to force schools to admit them.)

Many of the activists taking part in these protests were college students. Most were black Southerners, although they were strongly supported by Northern blacks and liberal whites. Thousands were arrested and jailed. Some were attacked and beaten. A few were murdered. Their efforts helped bring about the desegregation of public facilities in hundreds of Southern towns and cities.

In April 1963, Martin Luther King, Jr., and his associates began a campaign to desegregate public facilities in Birmingham, Alabama. Birmingham's black citizens, one third of the city's population of more than 350,000, were discriminated against in housing, restaurants, even in public parks. And Birmingham's police department, headed by the openly racist Eugene "Bull" Connor, was well known for brutality against blacks in general and for violent responses to peaceful protest in particular.

Through April and into May, hymn-singing protesters were beaten and arrested. Bull Connor's policemen turned firehoses and set police dogs on nonviolent demonstrators, many of them children. Americans across the country were horrified by the violence, which was broadcast on the national news. Meanwhile, negotiations were going on between black leaders and white businessmen and politicians. At the beginning of May, U.S. Attorney General Robert Kennedy sent a representative to Birmingham to press for peace. Finally, all the parties agreed on terms for desegregating and ending the protests.

"Birmingham has taught white America many lessons," Bayard Rustin, a civil rights leader, wrote at the time. ". . . Negroes will not wait another twenty-five years. . . . The Negro community is now fighting for total freedom. . . . The Negro masses are no longer prepared to wait for anybody. . . . They are going to move. Nothing can stop them from moving. And if that Negro leadership does not move rapidly enough and effectively enough they will take it into their own hands and move anyhow." [1]

In the weeks after the campaign in Birmingham, a wave of civil rights demonstrations—as well as many violent clashes between black activists and whites who opposed them—washed over the South. Thousands were arrested. In mid-June, the governor of Alabama, George Wallace, swore that he would personally prevent black students from enrolling at Alabama's previously all-white state university. (Wallace, during his successful 1962 election campaign and in his 1963 inaugural address, had promised Alabama voters "segregation now, segregation tomorrow, segregation forever.")

President John F. Kennedy took a firm stand on enforcing the federal court decision ordering that black students be allowed to attend the school. After National Guardsmen sent to the campus enabled two black students to register peacefully for classes, President Kennedy addressed the nation, on June 11:

> I hope that every American, regardless of where he lives, will stop and examine his conscience about this and other related incidents.
>
> This nation was founded by men of many nations and backgrounds. It was founded on the principle that all men are created equal, and that the rights of every man are diminished when the rights of one man are threatened. . . .
>
> It ought to be possible, therefore, for American students of any color to attend any public institution they select without having to be backed up by troops. It ought to be possible for American consumers of any color to receive equal service in . . . hotels and restaurants, and theaters and retail stores without being forced to resort to demonstrations in the street.

George Wallace, elected governor of Alabama in 1962, was an outspoken advocate of segregration. Here he stands with highway patrolmen blocking the doorway of a building of the University of Alabama, refusing to allow black students to enroll at the all-white university.

Medgar Evers, slain leader of the NAACP.

And it ought to be possible for American citizens of any color to register and to vote in a free election without interference or fear of reprisal.

It ought to be possible, in short, for every American to enjoy the privileges of being American without regard to his race or his color. . . .

The time has come for this nation to fulfill its promise. The events in Birmingham and elsewhere have so increased the cries for equality that no city or state or legislative body can prudently choose to ignore them. . . .

Next week I shall ask the Congress of the United States to act, to make a commitment it has not fully made in this century to the proposition that race has no place in American life or law. . . .

But legislation . . . cannot solve this problem alone. It must be solved in the homes of every American in every community across our country. . . .

This is a matter which concerns this country and what it stands for, and in meeting it I ask the support of all our citizens.[2]

Hours after Kennedy spoke, Medgar Evers, a Mississippi leader of the National Association for the Advancement of Colored People (NAACP), was shot to death outside his home by a white racist.

One week later, Kennedy sent his promised Civil Rights Bill to Congress.

Planning the March

Ralph Abernathy, a close associate of the Reverend Martin Luther King, Jr., later recalled that the idea for a march on Washington had been talked about among civil rights leaders for a long time. "Whenever we felt discouraged at the lack of progress in a local campaign," he said in his autobiography *And the Walls Came Tumbling Down*, "someone was bound to say, 'Why don't we just go up to Washington with as many people as we can muster, and tell Congress what we want face to face?'

"Everyone would nod and say, 'Maybe we ought to do that,' but we were always in the middle of some march or demonstration and had too many problems already without taking on another project."[1]

About the time of the 1963 Birmingham protests, however, black civil rights leaders began to talk more seriously about marching on Washington. A. Philip Randolph (who'd had the idea for a march on Washington in 1941) had already been making plans for a summertime march "for jobs and freedom," and in June, Randolph and the leaders of several civil rights organizations finally sat down to plan a march together. Randolph and these leaders became known as the "Big Six":

[23]

A. Philip Randolph, the elder statesman of the group.

Roy Wilkins, leader of the National Association for the Advancement of Colored People (NAACP). By 1963 the NAACP was the largest, best-known, and best-funded civil rights organization in the country. The NAACP, founded in 1909, was best known for pressing Congress and state legislatures for changes in laws discriminating against black Americans and for pursuing court cases against discrimination and segregation (including the 1954 *Brown* school desegregation case). Roy Wilkins, head of the NAACP since 1955, had worked for the organization since 1931.

Whitney Young, Jr., of the National Urban League. Founded in 1910 to help pave the way for Southern rural blacks migrating to cities in the North, the Urban League was well established, moderate, multiracial, and large. The Urban League, with branches in thirty states, had several hundred employees at its New York headquarters.

Martin Luther King, Jr., of the Southern Christian Leadership Conference (SCLC). King, by 1963 clearly the "star" of the civil rights movement after the Montgomery bus boycott, was one of the founders of the SCLC. The SCLC linked together black Southern ministers to sponsor nonviolent direct-action protests against discrimination.

John Lewis, newly elected head of the Student Nonviolent Coordinating Committee (SNCC, pronounced 'snick'). SNCC was created to organize protests by black and white students against discrimination throughout the South. In 1963, SNCC was a young organization with passionate members, many of whom had been beaten or jailed for participating in protests. (John Lewis, only twenty-three years old, had already been arrested dozens of times.)

James Farmer, a leader of the Congress of Racial Equality (CORE). Founded in Chicago in 1942, CORE was dedicated to using non-violent direct action to bring about racial integration. One of its efforts was to sponsor Freedom Riders seeking to desegregate interstate bus facilities in the South.

The NAACP and the National Urban League thought that CORE and especially SNCC were too militant, too radical. (The NAACP hadn't even wanted a march at first. They preferred a quieter, behind-the-scenes style of activism.) SNCC and CORE, for their part, thought that the more moderate groups were too polite and willing to compromise. Martin Luther King, Jr., and the SCLC tended toward the middle. A. Philip Randolph, greatly respected by all of the march organizers, acted as a peacemaker and unifier.

A final key figure in organizing the march was Bayard Rustin. Fifty-three years old in 1963, Rustin had spent his entire adult life organizing countless nonviolent antiwar and civil rights protests. He had helped Randolph plan the 1941 march on Washington and was deeply disappointed when Randolph canceled it. Rustin was the first person to whom Randolph turned for help with organizing the 1963 march.

Randolph wanted Rustin to be named chief organizer for the march, but other members of the Big Six thought Rustin was too controversial. As a young pacifist, Rustin had flirted with communism when the Communist party was opposing World War II. A lifelong Quaker, he had gone to jail as a conscientious objector instead of serving in the military during the war. And he had been arrested, in 1953, for having sex with consenting adult men. (Homosexual acts were not only illegal in many states at the time but also frequently targets for police action.)

Four members of The Big Six, the planners of the march. From left to right: Whitney Young, Roy Wilkins, James Farmer, John Lewis.

A. Philip Randolph, known as the grandfather of the civil rights movement, was president of the Brotherhood of Sleeping Car Porters, the first black union.

The NAACP's Roy Wilkins insisted on keeping Rustin out of the limelight. "Randolph wanted to make Bayard Rustin head of the march, but I opposed the idea," Wilkins later recalled. "I have always admired Rustin's organizational skill and brilliant mind, but I worried that some aspects of his radical past might provide ammunition for our enemies, who were doing all they could to attack the march.

"Randolph held his ground, so we worked out a compromise. Rustin did most of the work, but he had to stay in the background. History has attached the name of Reverend King to the march, but I suspect it would be more accurate to call it Randolph's march—and Rustin's."[2]

Rustin understood Randolph's vision. Rustin later wrote that Randolph saw the march as "marking the termination of the mass protest period—during which Negroes had destroyed the Jim Crow institutions in the South—and the inauguration of an era of mas-

Although because of his past activities some felt Bayard Rustin was too controversial to be the official organizer of the march, he played an essential role as A. Philip Randolph's assistant.

sive action at the ballot box designed to bring about new economic programs. Aware that the central problem Negroes faced was no longer simply one of *civil* rights but of *economic* rights—for the one would lack social substance without the other—he called for a March on Washington . . . to demand '*Jobs* and Freedom.' "[3]

In June, however, before Randolph could carry out his plans, President Kennedy sent Congress his proposed Civil Rights Bill. "In the minds of some people," Rustin said, "this [bill] became the main focus of the march." Kennedy's bill, which Congress would still be debating at the time of the march, proposed banning racial discrimination in public facilities, increasing protection for black voting rights, and strengthening the federal government's ability to enforce desegregation of public schools. For most of the march organizers, focusing Congress's attention on the Civil Rights Bill did become a key goal of the march.

The possibility of violence was a grave concern of the march planners, and particularly of Martin Luther King, Jr. "Martin and I were both worried about violence," Ralph Abernathy later recalled. "Martin had said, 'The Negro is shedding himself of his fear, and my real worry is how we will keep this fearlessness from rising to violent proportions.' He had also expressed to me his concern that with SNCC involved the march could easily provoke an incident that could lead to trouble. 'If that happens, Ralph,' he said, 'everything we have done in Birmingham will be wiped out in a single day.' "[4]

The march organizers feared that violence could be set off not only by SNCC and CORE, but also by other black activists who were even more radical. Chief among those was the Black Muslim leader Malcolm X, whose fiery speeches were attracting many followers and sympathizers in the black ghettos of Northern cities.

Malcolm X during a Black Muslim rally in New York City.

Later that year, talking about the sometimes violent racial clashes that flared across the country that spring and summer before the march, Malcolm X said:

> They were talking about how they were going to march on Washington, . . . march on the Senate, march on the White House, march on the Congress and tie it up, bring it to a halt, not let the government proceed. They even said they were going out to the airport and lay down on the runway and not let any airplanes land. I'm telling you what they said. That was revolution. That was revolution. That was the black revolution. It was the grass roots out there in the street. It scared the white man to death.[5]

Moderate black organizations held themselves up to white America as a less frightening alternative to Malcolm X. "Martin and the regular civil rights leaders were presenting to America our best face. Our nonviolent face," said the black actor and writer Ossie

Davis, who helped organize entertainers participating in the march. "And we wanted to show the world that we had no evil intentions against anybody. We just wanted to be included.

"But they also understood that America in spite of our reassurances would be frightened and hesitant to open the doors to black folks. So Malcolm, as the outsider, as the man they thought represented the possibilities of violence, was the counter that they could use. They would say to the powers that be, 'Look, here's Martin Luther King and all these guys. We are nonviolent. Now, outside the door if you don't deal with us is the other brother, and he ain't like us. You going to really have hell on your hands when you get to dealing with Malcolm. So it behooves you, white America, in order to escape Malcolm, to deal with us.' That was the strategy. And to some degree it worked."[6]

Months after the march, Malcolm criticized the march for being "co-opted," taken over by white people, specifically by President Kennedy. Malcolm said that Kennedy had tried to get the march organizers to call the whole thing off. Then, when that didn't work, he said, the President's people took it over and dictated who would march, when, and where.

> It's just like when you've got some coffee that's too black, which means it's too strong. What do you do? You integrate it with cream, you make it weak. But if you pour too much cream in it, you won't even know you ever had coffee. It used to be hot, it becomes cool. It used to be strong, it becomes weak. It used to wake you up, now it puts you to sleep. This is what they did with the march on Washington. They joined it. They didn't integrate it, they infiltrated it. They joined it, became a part of it, took it over. And as they took it over, it lost its militancy. It ceased to be angry, it ceased to be hot, it ceased to be uncompromising. . . . It was a sellout. It was a takeover.[7]

In fact, Kennedy did oppose the march at first. Kennedy wanted his Civil Rights Bill to pass, and any violence or disorder at the march would make passing the bill that much more difficult. When it became obvious that the march would go on whether they liked it or not, the Kennedy administration pressed the march leaders to discourage any civil disobedience (blocking entrances to the Capitol, for example) and to hold a peaceful rally somewhere in Washington *away* from Capitol Hill.

The march organizers agreed at the beginning of July that the marchers would gather at the foot of the Washington Monument and march less than a mile through the streets of Washington to a rally at the Lincoln Memorial—2 miles (3 kilometers) from the halls of Congress. Speeches at the rally would be kept short so that the marchers could start leaving Washington by 5 P.M.

Because President John Kennedy had a civil rights bill before Congress at that time, he was concerned that the march be a peaceful demonstration. Kennedy convinced march leaders to gather the crowd away from the halls of Congress.

The Kennedy administration worked hard to make sure that the march would go smoothly, and that everything possible would be done to allow the marchers to assemble safely and peacefully. The Justice Department helped coordinate plans for security with the Washington police. In addition, the march organizers recruited 2,000 unarmed parade marshals, many of them off-duty New York City policemen, and gave them special training in "nonviolent tactics" for dealing with any clashes that might break out the day of the march.

By the beginning of July, Bayard Rustin had set up march headquarters in a tiny office in New York's Harlem, with stations in Washington and elsewhere. The volunteers who did the real work of organizing the march worked hard. Rustin was a tough taskmaster. He had to be. They had only eight weeks until march day, August 28, 1963, to pull together not only the largest civil rights demonstration in U.S. history but by far the largest group of demonstrators of any kind ever to assemble in Washington. Their goal was to get at least 100,000 demonstrators into Washington for the march—then move them all out of town again before sundown, to avoid the possibility of a night of violence.

Later in July, the Big Six became the Big Ten when several white labor and church leaders were added to the march's organizing committee: Mathew Ahmann (Catholic Conference for Interracial Justice), Eugene Carson Blake (National Council of Churches), Rabbi Joachim Prinz (American Jewish Congress), and Walter Reuther (United Auto Workers).

Churches, white as well as black, were an important source of money and other forms of support for the march. Political parties, however, were not. The march organizers had decided that the march should be completely nonpartisan—they established a pol-

Walter Reuther, president of the United Auto Workers Union, became one of the white leaders on the march's organizing committee.

icy that they would not accept money or sponsorship from any political party. Nor would they look for or accept corporate sponsorship or any linkage of commercial items or activities to the march, even though they needed money. Instead, the march organizers raised money to pay for everything from office space to phone bills to chartered buses from contributions from individuals and charitable organizations, and from the sale of "March on Washington" buttons—thousands of them—at 25 cents apiece.

The Day of the March

4

As the day of the march approached, Roy Wilkins recalled, "there were times when Washington seemed paralyzed by fear. On march day, the business community closed shop. . . . Behind these jitters lay a ridiculous, ignorant fear of black Americans. At the time, most of white Washington couldn't tell the difference between the talk of a stomping Baptist preacher and the words of the wildest black nationalist. Washington seemed to think it faced an assault by tens of thousands of radicals."[1]

As it turned out, the Black Muslims, who were attending their annual convention, were the most radical of the black activists in Washington that week, and they chose to stay clear of the march entirely. The night before the march, Malcolm X, speaking with reporters, sounded more indifferent than angry: "I am not condemning or criticizing the march," he said, "but it won't solve the problems of black people."[2]

Finally, on the morning of the march, the marchers arrived in Washington, "all in a holiday mood," Ralph Abernathy recalled. "Of all the demonstrations we ever organized, the crowd at the March on Washington was the happiest and the least likely to cause trouble."[3] The marchers came by bus, by train, by plane, by car—even on roller skates. It was the largest group ever to assemble for a mass demonstration in the nation's capital. And it was one of the most peaceful groups ever assembled anywhere. Not a single serious violent incident broke out all day long.

"There had never been such a crowd," one marcher later said. "There were society women in new hats and old women in Sunday go-to-church black; there were bright young men . . . looking important and hurried, and lost; there were pretty girls and plain ones, priests, preachers, and rabbis, union members, seminarians, housewives and teachers." [4] Many of the marchers brought signs to carry at the march. "Must we wait 100 or 200 more years for equality?" one fourteen-year-old girl's sign read.

Marchers gathered at early-morning prayer breakfasts and church services all over the city. Soon, they were assembling at the base of the Washington Monument. An all-star cast entertained them while they waited for the march to begin: actor and entertainer Harry Belafonte, gospel singer Mahalia Jackson, folksingers Joan Baez, Odetta, and Peter, Paul, and Mary, actors Marlon Brando and Charlton Heston, author James Baldwin, baseball great Jackie Robinson, and others.

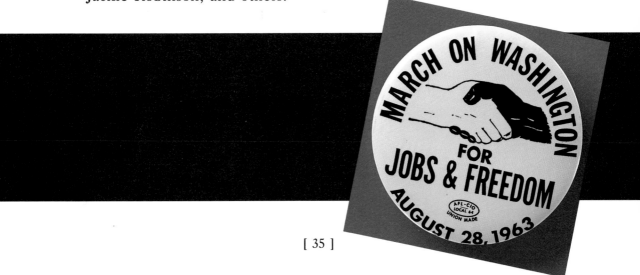

Although there were plenty of "stars" at the march, "it wasn't the Harry Belafontes and the greats from Hollywood that made the march," Bayard Rustin later said. "What made the march was that black people voted that day with their feet. They came from every state, they came in jalopies, on trains, buses, anything they could get—some walked." [5]

While the marchers were gathering at the Washington Monument, their leaders were on Capitol Hill, keeping appointments they had made with lawmakers there. "About 75 of us went to the offices of House and Senate leaders in both parties to ask for their support during the upcoming fight for passage of the president's civil rights bill," Ralph Abernathy later said. "They listened courteously to what we said and promised to give our words every consideration. I remember coming away with the idea that everyone was walking on eggs until after the march was over. Only then would they know for sure whether or not it was safe to say something positive about our visit." [6] All members of Congress were invited to the march, and chairs were set aside for them at the Lincoln Memorial.

While the march leaders were meeting with members of Congress, the marchers began to get impatient. Word reached Capitol Hill that the marchers were ready to march without their leaders, so the leaders scrambled to get across town to lead the march. As soon as they got there, the Big Ten linked arms at the front of the already moving line of marchers and set off on foot for the Lincoln Memorial.

Actually, there were two lines of marchers. One, the main group, was led by the Big Ten. Photographers and reporters and television film crews covered their progress from the Washington Monument to the Lincoln Memorial. (The march got more press coverage than any previous Washington event—more, even, than

Many actors, singers, and other celebrities entertained the marchers while they waited for the march to begin. Shown here, in front of the Lincoln Memorial, are actors Burt Lancaster, Harry Belafonte, and Charlton Heston.

Marchers link arms as they march for jobs and equal civil rights.

President Kennedy's glamorous inauguration two years before.) A secondary line of marchers following a different route was led by the wives of the march leaders.

None of the main scheduled speechmakers at the rally were women. No women were asked to attend the meeting with President Kennedy, scheduled for right after the rally. Some women involved in organizing the march had earlier voiced their dismay that the program did not reflect the importance of women in the civil rights movement. The all-male march leadership did not, however, make any changes in the program that would allow women to speak.

While the marchers marched, a last-minute controversy played out concerning the speech to be delivered by John Lewis, representing the Student Nonviolent Coordinating Committee (SNCC). Lewis's speech was the angriest and most militant speech of the day. As it was originally drafted, his speech began:

> We march today for jobs and freedom but we have nothing to be proud of. . . . In good conscience, we cannot support the Administration's civil rights bill, for it is too little, and too late. . . .
>
> I want to know—which side is the federal government on?
>
> The revolution is at hand, and we must free ourselves of the chains of political and economic slavery. . . .
>
> Mr. Kennedy is trying to take the revolution out of the streets and put it in the courts. Listen, Mr. Kennedy, listen. Mr. Congressman, listen, fellow citizens—the black masses are on the march for jobs and freedom, and we must say to the politicians that there won't be a "cooling-off period."
>
> We won't stop now. . . . The next time we march, we won't march on Washington, but will march through the South, through the Heart of Dixie, the way Sherman did. We will make the action of the past few months look petty. And I say to you, WAKE UP AMERICA![7]

Archbishop Patrick O'Boyle, the leader of Roman Catholics in the Washington area who was scheduled to deliver an opening prayer at the rally, had read an advance copy of Lewis's speech. He thought that it encouraged violence, and he was unwilling to be connected with it. According to Courtland Cox, a young SNCC organizer, "we got a message that Archbishop O'Boyle had stated that if we did not change John Lewis's statement, he was going to withdraw from the march. We told Bayard that you'd have to change the speech over our dead bodies."[8]

Fred Shuttlesworth, a preacher who had led demonstrations in Birmingham that year and who was at the march, later explained the feelings of some of Lewis's supporters about this: "I did not think it was necessary for John Lewis's speech to be changed. I didn't think we went up there to be little sweet boys. We were suffering. People were going to jail, people were dying and would be dying. So I didn't think we should gloss over that and act as if everything was pie in the sky, that we should be so thankful that we could come to Washington that we shouldn't say what was wrong with this country."[9]

In contrast, most of the march leaders were uncomfortable with at least the tone of Lewis's speech. In the end, A. Philip Randolph persuaded Lewis to change his speech for the sake of unity. According to Cox, Randolph told Lewis: " 'I have waited twenty-two years for this. Would you young men please accommodate an old man?' Randolph must have been about seventy-five, and here we were, one-third his age, and he was asking us to do this for him. He said, 'I've waited all my life for this opportunity. Please don't ruin it.' And we felt that, for him, we had to make some concessions."[10]

Lewis agreed not to directly attack the Kennedy administration and its civil rights bill. "It is true that we support the administration's Civil Rights Bill in the Congress," he agreed to say. "We support it with great reservations, however." Lewis also softened some of the speech's harsher language. He insisted, however: "To those who have said be patient and wait, we must say that we cannot be patient, we do not want our freedom gradually. For we want to be free now. . . . All over this nation, the black masses are on the march for jobs and freedom. They talk about slowing down and stop [sic]. We will not stop now."[11]

As it was actually delivered, even with the changes Lewis agreed to make, his speech was still the angriest and toughest talk of the day.

MARCH ON WASHINGTON FOR JOBS AND FREEDOM AUGUST 28, 1963

We Shall

Overcome

lomonaco

Official poster of the March on Washington.

At the Lincoln Memorial

While the last-minute rewriting of John Lewis's speech was still going on, the marchers were reaching their destination and filling up the park facing the Lincoln Memorial. Washington had never before seen such a huge crowd of demonstrators. Overall, it was a young crowd—about one sixth of the marchers were students. Although most of the marchers were black, one fourth of them were white. Most of the black marchers were from Northern cities rather than from the rural South, and many were well educated and politically active.

At 1:15 P.M., the rally got under way. "The Star-Spangled Banner" was sung, and Archbishop O'Boyle delivered his opening prayer. After several civil rights leaders and celebrities were briefly introduced to and applauded by the crowd, A. Philip Randolph got up to speak. Randolph, as expected, emphasized jobs as well as freedom.

> Fellow Americans, we are gathered here in the largest demonstration in the history of this nation. Let the nation and the world know the meaning of our numbers. We are not a pressure group. We are not an organization or a group of organizations. We are

[43]

not a mob. We are the advance guard of a massive moral revolution for jobs and freedom. . . .

We have taken our struggle into the streets as the labor movement took its struggle into the streets, as Jesus Christ led the multitudes through the streets of Judea. The plain and simple fact is that until we went into the streets the federal government was indifferent to our demands. It was not until the streets and jails of Birmingham were filled that Congress began to think about civil-rights legislation. It was not until thousands demonstrated in the South that lunch counters and other public accommodations were integrated, . . . and it was not until construction sites were picketed in the North that Negro workers were hired. . . .

The March on Washington is not the climax of our struggle but a new beginning, not only for the Negro but for all Americans who thirst for freedom and a better life. . . .

We here today are only the first wave. When we leave it will be to carry the civil-rights revolution home with us into every nook and cranny of the land and we shall return again and again to Washington in ever-growing numbers until total freedom is ours. We shall settle for nothing less and may God grant that we may have the courage, the strength, and faith in this hour of trial never to falter.[1]

After Randolph's speech, the program offered a brief tribute to the women in the civil rights movement, then entertainment by, among others, folksinger Bob Dylan. Eugene Carson Blake of the National Council of Churches spoke next, followed by SNCC's John Lewis. The crowd interrupted Lewis's controversial but brief speech fourteen times with great rounds of applause. After Lewis came another of the Big Ten, the well-known white labor leader Walter Reuther, who echoed many of Randolph's ideas, emphasizing that the civil rights movement was important not just to black

Americans but also to whites. "If we fail," he said, "the vacuum of our failure will be filled by the Apostles of Hatred who will search for answers in the dark of night, and reason will yield to riots, and brotherhood will yield to bitterness and bloodshed and we will tear asunder the fabric of American democracy."[2]

After Reuther finished his speech, Randolph returned to the podium to announce: "I am glad to report to you that the official count is that we have over 200,000 Negro and white workers" assembled at the Lincoln Memorial.[3] This was probably an underestimate. More likely, at least 250,000 and perhaps as many as 400,000 demonstrators participated in the march.

Next on the list of scheduled speakers was CORE's James Farmer. Farmer, however, was in jail for taking part in civil rights protests in Louisiana. He had decided that it wouldn't be right for CORE to bail him out of jail so that he could deliver his speech while his fellow protesters remained imprisoned. Floyd McKissick, another representative of CORE, read Farmer's speech to the crowd: "From a South Louisiana parish jail, I salute the March on Washington for Jobs and Freedom. Two hundred thirty-two freedom fighters here with me also send their greetings. I wanted to be with you with all my heart for this great day. I cannot come out of jail while they are still in, for their crime was the same as mine, demanding freedom now."[4]

The National Urban League's Whitney Young spoke to the crowd next. Young's speech focused on the unmet needs and unequal opportunities of blacks in the Northern cities:

They must march from the rat-infested, overcrowded ghettos to decent, wholesome, unrestricted residential areas dispersed throughout our cities. . . . They must march from the congested,

[45]

ill-equipped schools which breed dropouts and which smother motivation . . . and finally they must march from a present feeling of despair and hopelessness, despair and frustration, to a renewed faith and confidence. . . .

The hour is late, the gap is widening, the rumble of the drums of discontent resounding throughout this land are heard in all parts of the world.[5]

Mathew Ahmann of the Catholic Conference for Interracial Justice spoke next, followed by the NAACP's Roy Wilkins. Wilkins was obviously delighted at the huge number of people who had come to the march. "Isn't this a great day?" he said at the beginning of his speech. After greeting the crowd, he got down to business: "My friends, we are here today because we want the Congress of the United States to hear from us in person what many of us have been telling our public officials back home and, that is, *we want freedom now!*" Wilkins urged Congress to pass the Civil Rights Bill, and he outlined the need for making the law even stronger.

Wilkins urged the crowd to continue to put pressure on Congress: "Just by your presence here today we have spoken loudly and eloquently to our legislature. When we return home, keep up the speaking by letters and telegrams and telephone and, wherever possible, by personal visit. . . . My friends, you got religion here today. Don't backslide tomorrow."[6]

After Wilkins finished his speech, the great gospel singer Mahalia Jackson revived the heat-drowsy crowd with a dramatic delivery of the spiritual "I've Been 'Buked and I've Been Scorned." Rabbi Joachim Prinz of the American Jewish Congress spoke next. And then A. Philip Randolph went to the microphone once again, this time to introduce the most eagerly anticipated speaker of the day—the Reverend Martin Luther King, Jr. "I have

Gospel singer Mahalia Jackson.

the honor," Randolph said, "to present to you the moral leader of our nation."[7]

When King approached the podium, not only was he watched and listened to by the quarter of a million marchers assembled before him. His audience also included millions of television viewers. CBS had canceled its regular programming to cover the march all day long. When King began to speak, NBC and ABC, too, interrupted their regular programming to broadcast his speech. For the first time ever, civil rights had the entire nation's attention. Here's what King said:

I am happy to join with you today in what will go down in history as the greatest demonstration for freedom in the history of our nation.

Five score years ago, a Great American, in whose symbolic shadow we stand today, signed the Emancipation Proclamation. This momentous decree came as the great beacon light of hope for millions of Negro slaves who had been seared in the flames of withering injustice. It came as the joyous daybreak to end the long night of their captivity.

But one hundred years later the Negro still is not free. One hundred years later, the life of the Negro is still badly crippled by the manacles of segregation and the chains of discrimination. One hundred years later, the Negro lives on a lonely island of poverty in the midst of a vast ocean of material prosperity. One hundred years later, the Negro is still languished in the corners of American society and finds himself an exile in his own land. So we have come here today to dramatize the shameful condition.

In a sense we've come to our nation's capital to cash a check. When the architects of our republic wrote the magnificent words of the Constitution and the Declaration of Independence, they were signing a promissory note to which every American was to fall heir. This note was a promise that all men, yes, black men as well as white men, should be guaranteed the unalienable rights of life, liberty, and the pursuit of happiness.

It is obvious today that America has defaulted on this promissory note insofar as her citizens of color are concerned. Instead of honoring this sacred obligation, America has given the Negro people a bad check, a check which has come back marked "Insufficient Funds." But we refuse to believe the bank of justice is bankrupt. We refuse to believe that there are insufficient funds in the great vaults of opportunity of this nation. So we have come to cash this check, a check that will give us, upon demand, the riches of freedom and the security of justice. We have also come to this hallowed spot to remind America of the fierce urgency of now.

This is no time to engage in the luxury of cooling off or to take the tranquilizing drug of gradualism. Now is the time to make real the promises of democracy. Now is the time to rise from the dark and desolate valley of segregation to the sunlit path of racial justice. Now is the time to lift our nation from the quicksands of racial injustice to the solid rock of brotherhood. Now is the time to make justice a reality for all of God's children.

It would be fatal for the nation to overlook the urgency of the moment. This sweltering summer of the Negro's legitimate discontent will not pass until there is an invigorating autumn of freedom and equality. Nineteen sixty-three is not an end but a beginning. Those who hoped that the Negro needed to blow off steam and will not [sic] be content will have a rude awakening if the nation returns to business as usual. There will be neither rest nor tranquility in America until the Negro is guaranteed his citizenship rights. The whirlwinds of revolt will continue to shake the foundations of our nation until the bright day of justice emerges.

But there is something I must say to my people who stand on the warm threshold which leads them to the palace of justice. In the process of gaining our rightful place we must not be guilty of wrongful deeds. Let us not seek to satisfy our thirst for freedom by drinking from the cup of bitterness and hatred. We must forever conduct our struggle on the high plane of dignity and discipline. We must not allow our creative protest to degenerate into physical violence. Again and again we must rise to the majestic heights of meeting physical force with soul force.

The marvelous new militancy which has engulfed the Negro community must not lead us to a distrust of all white people, for many of our white brothers, as evidenced by their presence here today, have come to realize that their destiny is tied up with our destiny. They have come to realize that their freedom is inextricably bound to our freedom. We cannot walk alone.

And as we walk we must make the pledge that we shall always march ahead. We cannot turn back. There are those who are asking the devotees of civil rights: "When will you be satisfied?" We can never be satisfied as long as the Negro is the victim of the unspeakable horrors of police brutality. We can never be satisfied as long as our bodies, heavy with fatigue of travel, cannot gain lodging in the motels of the highways and the hotels of the cities. We cannot be satisfied as long as the Negro's basic mobility is from a smaller ghetto to a larger one. We can never be satisfied as long as our children are stripped of their selfhood and robbed of their dignity by signs stating: "For Whites Only." We cannot be satisfied as long as the Negro in Mississippi cannot vote and the Negro in New York believes he has nothing for which to vote. No, no, we are not satisfied and we will not be satisfied until justice rolls down like waters and righteousness like a mighty stream.

I am not unmindful that some of you have come here out of great trials and tribulations, some of you have come fresh from narrow jail cells, some of you have come from areas where your quest for freedom left you battered by the storms of persecution and staggered by the winds of police brutality. You have been the veterans of creative suffering. Continue to work with the faith that unearned suffering is redemptive.

Go back to Mississippi, go back to Alabama, go back to South Carolina, go back to Georgia, go back to Louisiana, go back to the slums and ghettos of our Northern cities, knowing that somehow this situation can and will be changed. Let us not wallow in the valley of despair.

I say to you today, my friends, even though we face the difficulties of today and tomorrow, I still have a dream. It is a dream deeply rooted in the American dream. I have a dream that one day this nation will rise up and live out the true meaning of its creed: "We hold these truths to be self-evident that all men are created equal." I have a dream that one day on the red hills of Georgia the sons of former slaves and the sons of former slave-owners will be able to sit down together at the table of brotherhood.

The Reverend Martin Luther King, Jr.,
delivering his now-famous
"I Have a Dream" speech to
the hundreds of thousands
of people gathered.

I have a dream that one day even the state of Mississippi, a state sweltering with the heat of injustice, sweltering with the heat of oppression, will be transformed into an oasis of freedom and justice. I have a dream that my four little children will one day live in a nation where they will not be judged by the color of their skin but by the content of their character. I have a dream today.

I have a dream that one day down in Alabama with its vicious racists, with its governor having his lips dripping with the words of interposition and nullification—one day right there in Alabama, little black boys and black girls will be able to join hands with little white boys and white girls as sisters and brothers.

I have a dream today.

I have a dream that one day every valley shall be exalted, every hill and mountain shall be made low, the rough places will be made plain and the crooked places will be made straight, and the glory of the Lord shall be revealed, and all flesh shall see it together.

This is our hope. This is the faith that I go back to the South with. With this faith we will be able to hew out of the mountain of despair a stone of hope. With this faith we will be able to transform the jangling discords of our nation into a beautiful symphony of brotherhood. With this faith we will be able to work together, to pray together, to struggle together, to go to jail together, to stand up for freedom together, knowing that we will be free one day.

This will be the day when all of God's children will be able to sing with new meaning: "My country 'tis of thee, sweet land of liberty, of thee I sing: Land where my fathers died, land of the pilgrims' pride, from every mountainside let freedom ring."

And if America is to be a great nation, this must become true. So, let freedom ring from the prodigious hilltops of New Hampshire. Let freedom ring from the mighty mountains of New York. Let freedom ring from the heightening Alleghenies of Pennsylvania. Let freedom ring from the snowcapped Rockies of Colorado. Let freedom ring from the curvaceous slopes of California. But not only that, let freedom ring from Stone Mountain of Georgia.

Let freedom ring from Lookout Mountain of Tennessee.

Let freedom ring from every hill and molehill of Mississippi. From every mountainside, let freedom ring. And when we allow freedom to ring, when we let it ring from every village, from every hamlet, from every state and every city, we will be able to speed up that day when all of God's children, black men and white men, Jews and Gentiles, Protestants and Catholics, will be able to join hands and sing in the words of the old Negro spiritual: "Free at last! Free at last! Thank God Almighty, we are free at last!" [8]

After the March

6

The program at the Lincoln Memorial ended soon after King's speech, shortly before 4:30 P.M. The organizers of the march had vowed to move all the marchers out of Washington by nightfall. And so they did.

The city emptied out. Bayard Rustin's volunteers cleaned up every scrap of litter left behind by the crowd. The March on Washington was over.

"I went back to the grounds [of the march] about six or seven o'clock that evening," Ralph Abernathy later remembered. "There was nothing but the wind blowing across the reflection pool, moving and blowing and keeping music. We were so proud that no violence had taken place that day. We were so pleased. . . .

This was the greatest day of my life." [1]

While the marchers were leaving Washington, the top march leaders met with President Kennedy at the White House for more than an hour. They talked mostly about the Civil Rights Bill. The President emphasized that the bill would need the strong support of Democrats and Republicans alike before it could become law.

Bayard Rustin believed that the march turned the tide in favor of civil rights in Congress. There were many congressmen at the march, Rustin later noted. Some stood on the sidelines; others sat in reserved areas. "And after they came and saw that it was very orderly, that there was fantastic determination, that there were all kinds of people there other than black people, they knew there was a consensus in this country for the civil rights bill."[2]

John F. Kennedy was shot to death by an assassin in November 1963. The following summer, Congress passed his Civil Rights Bill. In 1965, Congress passed a voting rights bill that greatly improved opportunities for Southern blacks actually to vote.

It's impossible to know exactly what role the 1963 March on Washington played in making the Civil Rights Bill and later civil rights legislation the law of the land. "I doubt that the March on Washington actually led to passage of the civil rights bill or, for the matter, to any other specific improvement in the condition of black Americans," Ralph Abernathy wrote years later in his autobiography. Nonetheless, Abernathy added, "Ceremonies of this sort have an important effect on the consciousness of a community or a people, even if they don't result in concrete actions. After the March on Washington, everyone felt better about themselves and about the country. We had gone to our nation's capital. We had not been unruly or even discourteous. Instead we had been joyously affirmative. We had staged a gigantic political rally—the largest of its kind in the history of the nation—and we had presented a gift to America, a great new affirmation of the principle of equality." He was referring to Martin Luther King's "I Have a Dream" speech.

"How he knew just what note to strike I can't say," Abernathy said. "It was part of his genius to be able to rise to such occasions and somehow transcend them. . . . Instead of dwelling on the bitterness of the past or the severe problems of the present he gave the cheering crowd, as well as the millions who watched on television, the vision of a future no one else had defined and few black people could imagine. It wasn't that Martin disagreed with the grim messages the others had brought to the crowd and to the American people. The dream he envisioned acknowledged the truth of everything that had already been said. He simply looked beyond the injustice and hatred and division to see what America could become, if and when it realized its fullest potential as a nation. It was a prophecy of pure hope at a time when black people and the nation as a whole needed hope more than anything else."[3]

On August 28, 1993, exactly thirty years to the day after the 1963 March on Washington, a crowd of approximately 75,000 gathered at the Lincoln Memorial to celebrate the anniversary of the great march and to push for "Jobs, Justice, and Peace." Veterans of the 1963 march were there, including Rosa Parks and Coretta Scott King, the widow of Martin Luther King, Jr.

John Lewis was there, too. By some measures, much progress had been made in the years since the 1963 march. In 1963, it was unthinkable that there could be a black congressman from Georgia. In 1993, John Lewis himself was representing Georgians in the U.S. House of Representatives. Also attending the celebration, living evidence of the political progress that African Americans had made, were Douglas Wilder, the nation's first black elected state governor, and Carol Moseley-Braun, the first black woman to serve in the U.S. Senate.[4]

In other ways, however, progress had not been made. Speakers pointed out that more poor black Americans than ever lived in miserable, violent ghettos with few opportunities for jobs at a living wage. What A. Philip Randolph had told President Kennedy about young black urban Americans after the march in 1963 was still true in 1993: "They have no faith in anybody white," he had said. "They have no faith in the Negro leadership. They have no faith in God. They have no faith in the government. In other words, they believe the hand of the society is against them."[5]

Two years later, on October 16, 1995, half a million African Americans gathered in Washington for a very different kind of march. Unlike the 1963 March on Washington, the 1995 Million Man March didn't seek to include white people (although a few white onlookers were present). Only black men were invited—black women were asked to stay home. Unlike the 1963 march, which demanded "Jobs and Freedom" for all, the 1995 march made most of its demands on the marchers, insisting that they should take more responsibility for themselves, their families, and their black communities.

The greatest difference between the two marches, however, was between the ideas and rhetoric of their leaders. Martin Luther King's vision was of a color-blind, integrated, tolerant America offering equal opportunity to all of its citizens. The leader of the 1995 march, Louis Farrakhan of the Nation of Islam, instead urged black Americans to tend to their own, separate, black communities. Martin Luther King, Jr., included "all of God's children" in his vision and his movement; Louis Farrakhan on many occasions had expressed bigoted sentiments against white people in general and Jews in particular. Martin Luther King, Jr., in his "I Have a

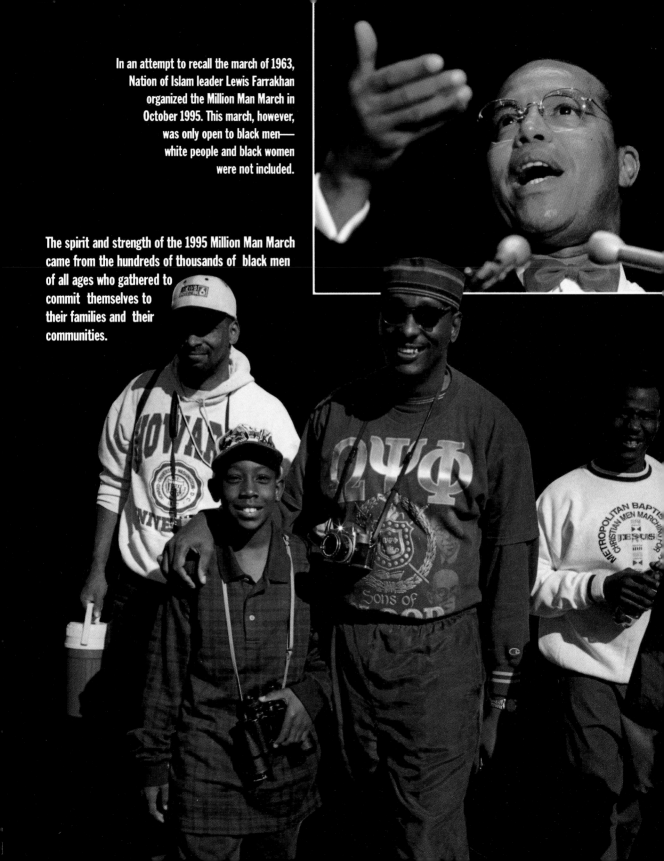

In an attempt to recall the march of 1963, Nation of Islam leader Lewis Farrakhan organized the Million Man March in October 1995. This march, however, was only open to black men—white people and black women were not included.

The spirit and strength of the 1995 Million Man March came from the hundreds of thousands of black men of all ages who gathered to commit themselves to their families and their communities.

Dream" speech, created in only a few minutes one of the most memorable and inspiring speeches of all time. During Louis Farrakhan's two-hour speech (delivered at the end of a twelve-hour rally), many of the marchers decided they'd had enough and headed home.

The marchers—not the leaders—were the most powerful feature of the Million Man March. Peaceful, relaxed, and confident, the hundreds of thousands of marchers had their minds on brotherhood and personal growth. When they left, they hoped to carry that spirit home with them. "I'm not here for Farrakhan," one marcher said. "I'm here to be a proud black man."[6]

Notes

The single most exhaustive source of information about the March on Washington is Thomas Gentile's *March on Washington: August 28, 1963* (Washington, DC: New Day Publications, 1983). Several other secondary sources figured prominently in the research for this book, especially C. Vann Woodward's *The Strange Career of Jim Crow*, second revised edition (New York: Oxford University Press, 1966) and Taylor Branch's *Parting the Waters: America in the King Years 1954–63* (New York: Simon and Schuster, 1988). Of all the major newspapers, *The New York Times* (August 29, 1963) offered the most thorough coverage of the march.

Introduction
"I Have a Dream"

1. Martin Luther King, Jr.'s march speech, reprinted in *The Cry for Freedom: An Anthology of the Best That Has Been Said and Written on Civil Rights Since 1954*, compiled and edited by Frank W. Hale, Jr. (New York: A. S. Barnes and Co., 1969), p. 371ff.

Chapter One
A Dream Deferred

1. Benjamin R. Tillman, excerpted in *Civil Rights and the American Negro: A Documentary History*, edited by Albert P. Blaustein and Robert L. Zangrando (New York: Washington Square Press, 1968), pp. 320–321.

Chapter Two
A Growing Movement

1. Bayard Rustin, introduction to a pamphlet, "Civil Rights: The True Frontier," June 18, 1963, reprinted in *Down the Line: The Collected Writings of Bayard Rustin* (Chicago: Quadrangle Books, 1971), p. 107ff.
2. Address by John F. Kennedy reprinted in *Let Freedom Ring: A Documentary History of the Modern Civil Rights Movement*, edited by Peter B. Levy (New York: Praeger, 1992), p. 117ff.

Chapter Three
Planning the March

1. Ralph David Abernathy, *And the Walls Came Tumbling Down* (New York: Harper & Row, 1989), p. 272.
2. Roy Wilkins with Tom Mathews, *Standing Fast: The Autobiography of Roy Wilkins* (New York: Viking Press, 1982), p. 292.
3. Bayard Rustin, "From Protest to Politics: The Future of the Civil Rights Movement," *Commentary* (February 1964), reprinted in *Down the Line*, p. 111ff.
4. Ralph David Abernathy, *And the Walls Came Tumbling Down*, p. 275.
5. November 1963 speech by Malcolm X, reprinted in *The Eyes on the Prize Civil Rights Reader: Documents, Speeches, and Firsthand Accounts from the Black Freedom Struggle, 1954–1990*, edited by Clayborne Carson et al. (New York: Viking, 1991), p. 248ff.
6. Ossie Davis, interview excerpted in *Voices of Freedom: An Oral History of the Civil Rights Movement from the 1950s through the 1980s*, by Henry Hampton et al. (New York: Bantam Books, 1990), pp. 162–163.
7. November 1963 speech by Malcolm X, reprinted in *Eyes on the Prize*, p. 248ff.

Chapter Four
The Day of the March

1. Roy Wilkins, *Standing Fast*, p. 292.
2. Malcolm X, quoted in *March on Washington*, p. 162.
3. Ralph David Abernathy, *And the Walls Came Tumbling Down*, pp. 277–278.

4. Lerone Bennet, quoted in *March on Washington*, p. 184.
5. Bayard Rustin, interview excerpted in *Voices of Freedom*, p. 169.
6. Ralph David Abernathy, *And the Walls Came Tumbling Down*, p. 278.
7. Draft (before editing) of John Lewis's march speech, reprinted in *Let Freedom Ring*, p. 120ff.
8. Interview with Courtland Cox, excerpted in *Voices of Freedom*, p. 164.
9. Interview with Fred Shuttlesworth, excerpted in *Voices of Freedom*, p. 167.
10. Interview with Courtland Cox, excerpted in *Voices of Freedom*, p. 164.
11. Speech as delivered, transcribed from audio recording, printed in *March on Washington: August 28, 1963*, pp. 180–181.

Chapter Five
At the Lincoln Memorial

1. A. Philip Randolph's march speech, reprinted in *Cry for Freedom*, p. 392ff.
2. Thomas Gentile, *March on Washington: August 28, 1963*, p. 228.
3. A. Philip Randolph, quoted in *March on Washington*, pp. 228–229.
4. James Farmer's march speech, quoted in *March on Washington*, p. 231ff.
5. Whitney Young's march speech, quoted in *March on Washington*, p. 232ff.
6. Roy Wilkins's march speech, reprinted in *Cry for Freedom*, p. 411ff.
7. A. Philip Randolph, quoted in *March on Washington*, p. 240.
8. Martin Luther King, Jr.'s march speech, reprinted in *Cry for Freedom*, p. 371ff.

Chapter Six
After the March

1. Interview with Ralph David Abernathy, excerpted in *Voices of Freedom*, p. 170.
2. Interview with Bayard Rustin, excerpted in *Voices of Freedom*, p. 169.
3. Ralph David Abernathy, *And the Walls Came Tumbling Down*, p. 281.
4. *The New York Times*, August 29, 1993.
5. Taylor Branch, *Parting the Waters*, p. 884.
6. *The New York Times*, October 17, 1995.

Further Information

Archer, Jules. *They Had a Dream: The Civil Rights Struggle, from Frederick Douglass to Marcus Garvey to Martin Luther King and Malcolm X*. New York: Viking, 1993.

Eyes on the Prize, a fourteen-part television series aired on PBS and produced by Blackside, Inc., 486 Shawmut Ave., Boston, MA 02118.

Haskins, James, with introduction by James Farmer. *The March on Washington*. New York: HarperCollins, 1993.

Haskins, Jim. *I Have a Dream: The Life and Words of Martin Luther King, Jr.* Brookfield, CT: Millbrook Press, 1992.

Levine, Ellen. *Freedom's Children: Young Civil Rights Activists Tell Their Own Stories*. New York: Putnam, 1993.

Index

Page numbers in *italics* refer to illustrations.

Abernathy, Ralph, 23, 28, 34, 36, 53, 54
Ahmann, Mathew, 32, 46
American Jewish Congress, 32
Armed forces, 14

Baez, Joan, 35
Baldwin, James, 35
Belafonte, Harry, 35, *37*
Big Six, 23-25, *26*, 32
Big Ten, 32, 36
Birmingham, Alabama, 19
Black Muslims, 28, 34
Blake, Eugene Carson, 32, 44
Boycotts, *17*, 18, 24
Brando, Marlon, 35
Brotherhood of Sleeping Car Porters, 16
Brown v. *Topeka Board of Education* (1954), 18, 24

Catholic Conference for Interracial Justice, 32
Civil Rights Bill of 1964, 22, 28, 31, 39, 41, 46, 53
Congress of Racial Equality (CORE), 25, 28, 45
Connor, Eugene "Bull," 19
Constitution of the United States, 12
Cox, Courtland, 40

Davis, Ossie, 29-30
Dylan, Bob, 44

Education, 11-12, 18
Evers, Medgar, *21*, 22

Farmer, James, 25, *26*, 45
Farrakhan, Louis, 56, *57*, 58
Freedom Riders, 18, 25

Gandhi, Mahatma, 18
Great Depression, 13, 16

Heston, Charlton, 35, *37*
Hughes, Langston, 10

Jackson, Mahalia, 35, 46, *47*
Jim Crow laws, 12, 18, 27

Kennedy, John F., 20, 22, 28, 30-31, *31*, 39, 41, 53, 54
Kennedy, Robert F., 19
King, Coretta Scott, 55
King, Martin Luther, Jr., *8*, 18, 19, 23-25, 27, 28, 30, 46, 47, *51*
   "I Have a Dream" speech, 9, 48-52, 54-56, 58

Lancaster, Burt, *37*
Lewis, John, 24, *26*, 39-41, 43, 44, 55
Linsey, John Lewis, 55
Lynching, 13, 14

Malcolm X, 28-30, *29*, 34
McKissick, Floyd, 45
Million Man March (1995), 56, *57*, 58
Montgomery, Alabama, *17*, 18, 24
Moseley-Braun, Carol, 55

National Association for the Advancement of Colored People (NAACP), 24, 25
National Council of Churches, *32*
National Urban League, 24, 25
Nation of Islam, 56
New Deal, 13-14
Nonviolence, 18, 29-30

O'Boyle, Patrick, 40, 43
Odetta, 35

Parks, Rosa, *17*, 18, 55
Peter, Paul, and Mary, 35
Plessy v. *Ferguson* (1896), 12
Prinz, Joachim, 32, 46

Randolph, A. Philip, 16, 23-25, *26*, 27-28, 40, 43-47, 56
Reuther, Walter, 32, *33*, 44-45
Robinson, Jackie, 35
Roosevelt, Franklin D., *14*, 14, 16
Rustin, Bayard, 19-20, 25, *27*, 27-28, 32, 36, 40, 53, 54

School desegregation, 18, 20, 24, 28
Segregation, 11-15, 18
"Separate but equal" doctrine, 12
Shuttlesworth, Fred, 40
Southern Christian Leadership Conference (SCLC), 24, 25
Student Nonviolent Coordinating Committee (SNCC), 24, 25, 28, 39
Supreme Court of the United States, 12, 18

Thirteenth Amendment to the Constitution, 11
Tillman, Benjamin R., 12-13

United Auto Workers, 32
University of Alabama, *21*

Voting rights, 12, 15, 28
Voting Rights Act of 1965, 54

Wallace, George, 20, *21*
Wilder, Douglas, 55
Wilkins, Roy, 24, *26*, 27, 34, 46

Young, Whitney, Jr., 24, *26*, 45-46